YOUR KNOWLEDGE HAS

Georg Trenovski

Performance of Cloud Based Solutions. The Impact of Public Cloud, Private Cloud and Hybrid Cloud

GRIN Publishing

Bibliographic information published by the German National Library:

The German National Library lists this publication in the National Bibliography; detailed bibliographic data are available on the Internet at http://dnb.dnb.de .

Imprint:

Copyright © 2014 GRIN Verlag GmbH
Print and binding: Books on Demand GmbH, Norderstedt Germany
ISBN: 978-3-656-93019-8

This book at GRIN:

http://www.grin.com/en/e-book/294956/performance-of-cloud-based-solutions-the-impact-of-public-cloud-private

GRIN - Your knowledge has value

Since its foundation in 1998, GRIN has specialized in publishing academic texts by students, college teachers and other academics as e-book and printed book. The website www.grin.com is an ideal platform for presenting term papers, final papers, scientific essays, dissertations and specialist books.

Visit us on the internet:

http://www.grin.com/

http://www.facebook.com/grincom

http://www.twitter.com/grin_com

Performance of Cloud Based Solutions
The Impact of
Public Cloud, Private Cloud &
Hybrid Cloud

RESEARCH BASED THESIS

Empiric Method: Theoretically

Bachelorstudium

"Management, Communication & IT"

Management Center Innsbruck

person in charge: Kristof Schneider

Responsibility:

2014

Georg Trenovski

Date (2014-01-30)

Table of Contents

Pictures

Abbreviations

API	Application programming interface
CRM	Customer Relationship Management
ETSI	European Telecommunications Standards Institute
IAAS	Infrastructure as a Service
PAAS	Platform as a Service
NIST	National Institute for Standards and Technologie
SAAS	Software as a Service
SLA	Service Level Agreement
SOA	Service Orientated Architecture
VM	Virtual Machine

1   Introduction

The cloud paradigm introduces a change in visualization of system and data owned by an enterprise. Further, the on service-based sharing of resources such as storage, hardware and applications which are delivered with cloud computing in a total different way has facilitated coherence of the resources and economies of scale through its pay-per-use business model. It is no longer a collection of devices on a physical location and run a particular software program with all the needed data and resources present at a physical location but instead is a system which is geographically distributed with consideration on both application and data. But even when the development of distributed cloud architectures and services are all dealing with the same issues of scalability, elasticity over demand, broad network access, usage measurement, security aspects such as authorization and authentication, and many other concepts related to multitenant services in order to serve a high number of concurrent users over the internet, is it the main goal for companies to find the right solution for their requiernents. The right solution can be a public, a private or a hybrid cloud and although the issues are very similar in any of these solutions, it depends further on the degree of potency of one or some issues which are related to different kind of industries and organisations to evaluate the right cloud based approach for a particular company. This means we have to agree that the evolution of a new paradigm requires adaptation in usage patterns and associated functional areas to fully benefit from the paradigm shift.

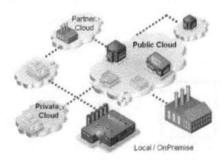

Abbildung 1: Which one is the best Solution?
(Kirstof Schneider Trends in BI)

1.1   Definition: Cloud Computing

Researchers and engineers working in the field of cloud computing define it in many ways. These definitions are usually based on the application's perspective, that is, the way one is trying to employ cloud services for a particular application. A few definitions of cloud computing are as shown below:

- *Cloud computing is a model for enabling convenient, on demand network access to a shared pool of configurable computing resources (e.g., networks, servers, Storage, applications, and services) that can be rapidly provisioned and released with minimal management effort or service provider interaction.*

- *A Cloud is a type of parallel and distributed system consisting of a collection of interconnected and virtualized computers that are dynamically provisioned and presented as one or more unified computing resources based on service-level agreements established through negotiation between the service provider and consumer.* (Mahmood 2013: 54)

1.2   Characteristics of Cloud Systems

General Characteristics of Cloud computing are as follows:

On-demand self-service: A consumer can unilaterally provision computing capabilities, such as server time and network storage, as needed automatically without requiring human interaction with each service provider.

Broad network access: Capabilities are available over the network and accessed through standard mechanisms that promote use by heterogeneous thin or thick client platforms (e.g. mobile phones, tablets, laptops and workstations).

Resource pooling: The provider's computing resources are pooled to serve multiple consumers using a multi-tenant model, with different physical and virtual resources dynamically assigned and reassigned according to consumer demand. There is a sense of location independence in that the customer generally has no control or knowledge over the exact location of the provided resources but may be able to specify location at a higher level of abstraction (e.g. country, state or data centre). Examples of resources include storage, processing, memory and network bandwidth.

Rapid elasticity: Capabilities can be elastically provisioned and released, in some cases automatically, to scale rapidly outward and inward commensurate with demand. To the consumer, the capabilities available for provisioning often appear to be unlimited and can be appropriated in any quantity at any time.

Measured service: Cloud systems automatically control and optimise resource usage by leveraging a metering capability at some level of abstraction that is appropriate to the type of service used (e.g. storage, processing, bandwidth and active user accounts). Resource usage can be monitored, controlled and reported, providing transparency for both the provider and consumer of the utilised service. (Mahmood 2013: 56)

2 A Cloud Solution: Requirement & Assessment

To truly benefit from cloud environment, software development teams should look at the cloud computing environment as a new development paradigm and leverage it to lead to differentiated value. The rest of the chapter explains positioning of the application development process to enable to take the advantage of the distributed nature of cloud environment. It answers the question of readiness regarding to the implementation of a cloud service in an organisation. (Mahmood 2013: 80)

2.1 Requirement Analysis

The industry, in general, tends to think of cloud as an enabler or rather a solution and hence believes that it has no bearing on requirements. The truth is that cloud is more of a choice at enterprise level. Hence, the fitment of the choice is an important aspect of the analysis phase. Along with the choice, the guidelines and checklists that aid in requirement analysis are also required for applications moving to cloud to be successful. The requirement analysis needs to address this assessment. These relevant requirements are mostly non-functional in nature. This implies the following additional tasks that need to be planned as part of requirement analysis:

- Cloud assessment
- Cloud usage pattern identification and capturing data points to support requirement analysis based on usage patterns (Mahmood 2013: 80)

2.1.1 The cost of non-functional Requirment

"As cloud computing is methodology of using tools and accessing applications from the Internet, cloud computing always reduces IT cost is a general misconception everyone has. The success of cloud computing vendors also depends on pricing. In general, while cloud computing provides cost savings for enterprises when setting up initial infrastructure, running costs and other operational costs may negate the initial savings enterprises make. But it is always suggestible to compare the initial cost of setup with an on-premise option with the cost per month cloud option and then evaluate the cloud migration strategy. Costing

on cloud is of type of pay-per-use model. The service providers charge separately on multiple factors like number of instances, bandwidth, load balancing, transaction volume, and other factors". (Mahmood 2013: 81)

2.2   Cloud Assessment

Cloud readiness assessment will help to evaluate the cloud readiness and applicability for an enterprise. The assessment also helps to determine the business case and return on investment. Typical assessment questions are listed below for reference. Note that this list is not exhaustive:

- Does cloud architecture fit the requirements for the application?
- How interconnected is this application with other application in the enterprise—for public cloud, can these interfaces be exposed for access from external networks?
- Is the enterprise comfortable with public cloud, or should the enterprise focus only on private cloud option among other options?
- Identifying suitable cloud service provider (IAAS/PAAS [2]—and the specific vendor under the category)
- Defining the strategy in adopting cloud for future projects
- Assessing the cost of using cloud (private or public cloud) (compare—capital expense of hosted option vs. running cost of cloud option)
- How would applications be monitored after they are hosted on public cloud?

It is important to note that cloud assessment guidelines are defined at enterprise level. The enterprise can optionally create tools to aid the projects and new initiatives to perform cloud assessment. (Mahmood 2013: 81)

3   The Favour of Cloud Computing

The terms Cloud computing and Cloud services are various used for many things, but in the general sense it means that a application or a service is used over the internet where users subscribe to a set of services rathern than consummate a service implementation. The European Telecommunications Standards Institute (ETSI) emphasize of the need of Interoperability between the offerings of different cloud providers. This means that solutions should be able to orchestrate software and data hosts from more than one cloud infrastucture, this capability was designate by Cisco with the term "intercloud" in analogy to the internet.

For that reason it is also expedient to define APIs and SLAs to be on the safe side. The ETSI also mentioned: *"Software licensing is a major inhibitor of the adoption of flexible computing models, including cloud infrastructure services. Cost savings in hardware, IT infrastructure management and energy can be negated by the need to purchase in advance, sufficient licenses to cover the maximum size of an application deployment."*

To display the current cloud environment correctly it is first necessary to draw a line between public cloud and private cloud. The distinctions are explained in this Chapter below. (Missbach 2013: 8)

3.1 Public Cloud

A public cloud is always in the possession of a service provider, this provider take care about the operation of the service and make it available for many users - business or individual. A public cloud can be imaging as a highly integrated data center with thousands of computers and mass storage pools. Cloud Fabric controllers are software components in these cloud infrastructures which maintain the life cycle of services – from the creation to deletion – and monitoring performance, availability and compliance with the SLAs. Important distinctions from the classic offerings of hosting providers and outsourcers are the principles of pay-per-use and the fact that resources can be requested and released literally at any time. This on-demand and pay-per-use approach offers significant advantages for service consumers, who doesn't need to incur the capital cost of investing in new servers and can react flexible, to respond to changing business conditions. By massive automation, the use of pools of compute, storage and network resources and economies of scale, public cloud providers can offer their services for extreme low prices. Besides "full service" clouds there are cloud providers like Apple's iCloud or Dropbox who focus on convenient storage space only. It is expected that the range of cloud services will increase in the future by new vendors offering specific cloud resources for specific target markets. (Missbach 2013: 9)

3.1.1 Anything as a Service

Two ways to utilize public clouds are popular but often confused: Infrastructure as a Service (IaaS) and Platform as a Service (PaaS).

- **IaaS example: Amazon Web Services (AWS)**
  Amazon Web Services (AWS) is a typical example for IaaS. AWS provide server, network and storage resources and give the customer the choice of Windows or Linux as operating system. The virtual environments available through AWS behave exactly like a local infrastructure, so customers configure the infrastructure according to the demand of any specific application. Such access to the configuration is a mandatory demand for the installation of SAP NetWeaver

solutions and the SAP Business suite. However the customer is also responsible for all admin tasks like patching or configuring the Operating System.

- **PaaS example: Windows Azure**

  A typical example for PaaS is Windows Azure. In such a setup, the customers have not to deal with admin tasks like patching or configuring the Operating System which are maintained by the cloud fabric controller. The advantage of this model is less effort required for the administration of the cloud platform. The disadvantage is that a customer has no control over the operating system in a VM, as this part has been delegated to the cloud fabric controller. While applications like web servers deal well with this model, many applications – especially those heavyweights like SAP NetWeaver – do require control over the operating system during installation and operation. As a consequence, applications that are scheduled to be run in the PaaS model need to be developed and adapted for this environment. However, the probability that SAP will reworks the technical basis for their Business Suite based on the SAP NetWeaver stack for this model is highly unlikely. (Missbach 2013: 9)

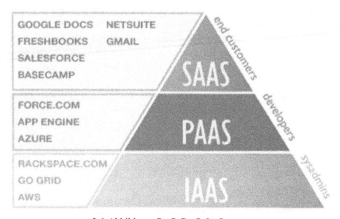

3-1 Abbildung: SaaS, PaaS, IaaS
(Goran Čandrlić)

3.2   Cloud Applications - Software as a Service

Applications which are exclusively made available by the vendor over the internet are called as Software as a Service (SaaS). Users of SaaS don't have to think neither how the application is installed and maintained nor how the data is stored or otherthings in regards of the operating system or the hardware. There is only one important thing you they have to place to the SaaS vendor and this is the trust that their sensitive data like the core financial situation of their company, the credit card numbers of their customers or the salaries of their workforce is kept save in the datacenter of the SaaS vendor and the mission critical application is always available. (Missbach 2013: 10) The SaaS vendor exploits the economies-of-scale available from sharing resources and services between multiple tenants, whilst the SaaS tenant benefits from low start-up-cost and quick return-on-investment. SaaS is not a software construction model but a software delivery model. Service Oriented Architecture (SOA) provides a suitable software construction model for SaaS. As such, a SaaS application can be exposed as a service and delivered to a variety of tenants. In addition, a SaaS vendor can outsource certain functionalities of its SaaS application to third party services (partner services) and can bind/unbind them depending on fluctuating demand, making it a dynamic service composition (Salinesi 2013: 338). A prominent example of SaaS is the company Salesforce.com who offering a CRM solution as a Service. Other examples are Google or Microsoft such as Microsoft Dynamics CRM SaaS. SAP announced Sales OnDemand (CRM) as their first SaaS type solution already in 2006. The ERP solutions SAP Business byDesign (ByD) became available 2010 as the first solution from SAP developed from the ground up as a cloud application, followed by Carbon Impact OnDemand (sustainability), Sourcing OnDemand, and Travel OnDemand (expense reporting). One of the biggest benefits of ByD is that it can be used with very little customization, enabling extreme fast implementation. However this is also the biggest drawback, because it also didn't allow customizing of the solution according to customer demands.

A special category are hybrid solutions like SAP x-Apps which can be composed of SaaS application and application residing on premises using the web services paradigm. The co-existence of best-of-breed talent management solutions (typically SaaS) alongside core HR (typically on-premises) is also quite common.

3.2.1 Differences between Classical ERP Systems and SaaS Systems

"The major differences between the classical ERP system and the investigated SaaS solution are the customizability of the ERP solution and the concomitant effect on the implementation expenses and in further consequence on the total costs of ownership (TCO)". (Piazolo 2013: 173)

- **Customizability**
  The customizability of the new solution differs from the classical ERP customizability because of its business orientation. That means the user doesn't require any technical know-how in order to configure the system. The technical system configurations are made automatically by the system in the background. Regarding this business oriented customizability the following advantages are stated.
  - o Simplification of the configuration process due to the central configuration for the entire system and the possibility to configure the system in each product lifecycle stage.

o   High transparency through disclosure of the entire range of functions in the solution catalogue.

o   Users establish their own solution, with a maximum of control of the implementation by the use of commercial language and without necessity of technical specialized knowledge.

- **Cost**

  The TCO of a SaaS model can decrease, in comparison to that one of a classical ERP system, according toMathewandNairover a period of 3 years around up to 60 %. In order to verify this statement it requires of a more exact calculation which must be carried out individually for a company in each case for classical ERP and SaaS solution. (Piazolo 2013: 174)

Table 1 Properties, reasons and impact on costs

Properties of SaaS solution	Reasons	Impact on costs
Fast availability	Enabled through the access via internet	Potential to reduce the implementation costs
Lower training expenditure	By intuitive user interface and product innovation in the area of integrated learning environment	Reduction of the training expenses
Simplified configuration	By predefined functions and processes within the Business Adaption Catalogue	Reduction of the implementation expenses and the duration, reduction of consultant's expenses
Predefined functions and processes	Potentials out of using best practice processes	Reduction of development and implementation costs
Outsourcing of the IT infrastructure	New technology "cloud"	Reduction of the IT personnel expenses, the hardware and software costs, and the current operation costs
Flexible extensibility of the solution	Modular structure of the solution's extent	Reduction of the monthly royalty based on the solution's extent

3-2 Abbildung: Impact of SaaS
(Piazolo 2013: 175)

3.3   Private Cloud

In opposite to the public cloud solutions are private clouds infrastuctures made for the use for a specific organisation. For that reason it is also very common that the company owns data center is the also the hoster of the private cloud which takes further the responibility for the operation by their own IT organization.

3.3.1   On Premise

This way, sensitive data can be kept within the company and control of the data and processes is secured. Consequently, legal or security aspects of handling such data do not need to be considered and audited, representing the major advantage of the private cloud. But private clouds are not limited to on-premises operations in a company. Ironically private clouds can be also provided as a service from a public cloud provider, however exclusively for a specific customer. (Missbach 2013: 11)

3.3.2   Off Premise

In this case the infrastructure is not set up as a multi-tenant architecture but as single-tenant architecture to minimize the risk of "intra-cloud" attacks. In order to build private cloud solutions, building blocks for hardware and software can be combined in a modular fashion. Hardware vendors such as Cisco in partnership with VMware and EMC or NetApp for example, offer pre-configured and SAP-certified building blocks with carefully optimized combinations of server, virtualization and storage infrastructures "ready to run" for private clouds (Vblock or Flexpod). This infrastructure can be combined with cloud-controllers and automation software, for example SAP LVM. (Missbach 2013: 11)

3.3.3   Private Cloud Opportunities and Challenges

While the public cloud's infrastructure can presumably be used most efficiently, it may not be the best choice. Interest in private cloud solutions has grown tremendously in the last several years. An IEC study (2011: The cloud computing shift: from custom-built to commodity hosting. The Corporate Executive Board Company) of projected public and private cloud adoption found that continued uncertainty regarding the potential risks of the public cloud will drive private cloud investment. The private cloud delivery model justifies its premium by providing more control than the public cloud allows. Unlike the public cloud, a private cloud offers greater ability to customize and share infrastructure, albeit at a higher cost (ultimately, private cloud providers and consumers give up some of the cost benefits inherent to the public cloud; for reasons related to scale, automation capabilities, and people/organizational skills, it is simply not possible to provide private cloud services as inexpensively as public cloud services) (Missbach 2013: 192)

3.4   Hybrid Cloud: Gathering the Best

NIST - National Institute for Standards and Technologie views a hybrid as a combination of public and private clouds, but practical experience and the popular press include mixing in traditional platforms as well. Organizations might wish to maintain their critical ERP system in their own datacenter atop a private cloud and deploy non-critical parts on a public cloud infrastructure. Deploying non-production systems such as training, business sandboxes, and pilot systems (that do not hold sensitive data) on the public cloud could reduce ongoing infrastructure costs without incurring significant risks. Integrating these different systems into the transport management system add some complexity and administration effort. Assuming business functionality and risks are within acceptable limits, though, designing such a hybrid cloud solution for SAP or any other system could make drive significant cost reductions. Finally, a hybrid SAP architecture for example could be deployed that seamlessly integrates internally hosted capacity (such as a system's SAP CRM web application servers) with other cloud-based application servers that can be quickly spun up and spun back down. Such "cloud bursting" or "renting the peak" would reduce the system's fixed costs while enhancing its flexibility and ability to meet unknown peak demands. Of course, the potential network latency and application performance implications are tremendous, necessitating thorough load testing to confirm that the bursting process indeed delivers at the necessary service levels. More realistically, a company might initially use such a bursting strategy to address batch workload or other asynchronous processing needs. Once the network and integration framework tying together private and public resources is proven in the real world, using it to deliver real-time computing would eventually become more realistic. In all three cases, the potential to reduce overall ERP system landscape costs and increase business agility may outweigh the risks and other tradeoffs, making a hybrid cloud solution an ideal (albeit limited) interim state for SAP customers. (Missbach 2013: 193)

4   Data & Security Consideration

"Data considerations include more than country-specific laws and regulations. Data can also be considered too sensitive to be hosted outside of the confines and control of an organization. If may be physically or logically difficult to access. High quality or sufficient bandwidth may be unavailable in certain geographic locations. Finally, the amount of data or the monthly growth in data might preclude effectively hosting data in a location that's sensitive to network latency, impacting the ability to consistently or legally access the data in a timely manner. Safeguarding corporate and customer data is only the tip of the iceberg. The growing number of legal compliance requirements, the ability to audit data trails, and safeguarding that data as it's moved between secured sites all conspire to create a complex web of challenges". (Missbach 2013: 200)

5   Conclusion / Solution

When we talk about *public cloud*, we mean that the whole computing infrastructure is located on the premises of a cloud computing company that offers the cloud service. The location remains, thus, separate from the customer and he has no physical control over the infrastructure. As public clouds use shared resources, they do excel mostly in performance, but are also most vulnerable to various attacks.

Private cloud means using a cloud infrastructure (network) solely by one customer/organization. It is not shared with others, yet it is remotely located. If the cloud is hosted extern the companies have an option of choosing an on-premise private cloud as well, which is more expensive, but they do have a physical control over the infrastructure. The security and control level is highest while using a private network. Yet, the cost reduction can be minimal, if the company needs to invest in an on-premise cloud infrastructure

Hybrid cloud, of course, means, using both private and public clouds, depending on their purpose. For example, public cloud can be used to interact with customers, while keeping their data secured through a private cloud. (Goran Čandrlić 2013)

The paper shows where the strenghes, weaknesses, challenges and opportunitys of the different cloud solutions are placed. Finally we draw a picture which businesses or individuals should use which cloud infrastructure:

- **Public Cloud**

  Students and Private Users as well as small companys with non confidential data can use Public Cloud services for data storage

  - o in the Ownership of an IT service located and from this powered Cloud environment
  - o Access via the Internet
  - o Flexible and quick use by subscription
  - o Provides a selection of high -standardized Business processes, applications and / or infrastructure services on a variable "Payper use" basis only

- **Private Cloud**

  A Private Cloud is the right solution for organisations on a global parquett who are using ERP or CRM services as well as have the desire to store customer data and other confidental datasets. Also medical organisations who are dealing with medical data should use a private cloud solution.

  - o Customer-specific, from customers themselves powered cloud environment
  - o Limited access and only for the customers themselves, authorized business partners, customers and Suppliers.

- o Efficient, standardized and safe IT operating environment under control of customers, the customization allowed.
- o Acess via intranet

- **Hybrid Cloud**

  In reality, primarily for the foreseeable future mixed forms (Hybrid clouds) will be used. Hybrid clouds are possible use combinations of Private clouds, Public clouds and traditional IT environment, the challenge will be to traditional IT environment, Private Cloud and / or Public Cloud to of the application, the middleware and infrastructure plane with respect to services and to integrate security so that a heterogeneous environment for the user is homogeneous.

References

Goran Čandrlić: Cloud Computing – Types of Cloud. URL:
   http://www.globaldots.com/wordpress/wp-
   content/uploads/2013/03/pas_ias_sas.png.
Mahmood, Z. & Saeed, S. (2013): Software Engineering Frameworks for the Cloud
   Computing Paradigm. London: Springer.
Missbach, M., Stelzel, J., Gardiner, C., Anderson, G. & Tempes, M. (2013): SAP on
   the Cloud. Berlin, Heidelberg: Springer.
Piazolo, F. & Felderer, M. (2013): Innovation and Future of Enterprise Information
   Systems: ERP Future 2012 Conference, Salzburg, Austria, November 2012,
   Revised Papers (2. Aufl.). s.l: Springer-Verlag.
Salinesi, C., Norrie, M. C. & Pastor, Ó. (2013): Advanced information systems
   engineering: 25th international conference, CAiSE 2013, Valencia, Spain, June
   17 - 21, 2013 ; proceedings. Berlin: Springer.